THE LITTLE REFUSES TO SURVIVE

60

AND BEYOND
by Aubrey Dillon Malone

Published in the UK by
POWERFRESH Limited
21 Rothersthorpe Crescent
Northampton
NN4 8JD

Telephone   0845 130 4565
Facsimile   0845 130 4563
E Mail   info@powerfresh.co.uk

Copyright © 2002 Aubrey Dillon Malone
Cover Nathan Cox
and interior layout by Powerfresh

ISBN 1902929284

Printed in Malta by Gutenberg Press Ltd
Powerfresh July 2002

I'm pleading with my wife to have birthdays again. I don't want to grow old alone.
(Rodney Dangerfield)

From birth to 18 a girl needs parents. From 18 to 35 she needs good looks. From 35 to 55 she needs a good personality. From 55 on, she needs good cash.
(Sophie Tucker)

As an Honours graduate of the Zsa Zsa Gabor School of Creative Mathematics, I honestly do not know how old I am.
(Erma Bombeck)

Mickey Rooney has to live to be 100 so he can pay the alimony he owes all those ex-wives. He's not ALLOWED to die.
(George Burns)

I'm pleased to be here.
Let's face it, at my age I'm
pleased to be anywhere.
(Ronald Reagan)

On my 70th birthday I hung a black wreath on my door.
(Bette Davis)

Yes, I'd consider going out with women my age -if there WERE any.
(George Burns at 92)

I've been around so long I knew Doris Day before she was a virgin.
(Groucho Marx)

I have my 87th birthday coming up and people are asking me what I'd like for it. I always answer a paternity suit.
(George Burns)

If you survive long enough
you're revered - rather like an
old building.
(Katharine Hepburn)

Advanced old age is when you sit in a rocking chair and can't get it going.
(Eliakim Katz)

When I started in show business, the Dead Sea was only sick.
(George Burns)

Old age is the happiest time in a man's life. The trouble is, there's so little of it.
(W.S. Gilbert)

I have no views. When one is retired it is sensible to refrain from having views,
(Joseph Alsop)

For a while you're venerable;
then you're, just old
(Lance Alworth)

It's not how old you are, it's how hard you work at it.
(Jonah Barrington)

Old age is always 15 years older
than what I am
(Bernard Baruch)

The trouble is, you're not allowed to grow old in the world anymore
(Tony Hancock)

Old age isn't so bad when you consider the alternative.
(Maurice Chevalier)

Old age takes away what we've inherited and gives us what we've earned.
(Gerald Brennan)

The worst thing anybody ever
said about me is that I'm 60.
Which I am.
(Joan Rivers)

You can calculate Zsa Zsa
Gabor's age by the rings on her
fingers
(Bob Hope)

If you live to be 100 you've got it made. Very few people die past that age.
(George Burns)

Growing old is like being increasingly penalised for a crime you haven't committed.
(Anthony Powell)

One of the good things about getting older is that you find you're more interesting than most of the people you meet.
(Lee Marvin)

I've reached the age where, when I see a pretty girl nowadays it arouses my memory instead of my hopes (Milton Berle)

Bob Hope is so old, when he first started going to school, history wasn't even a subject.

The four stages of man are
infancy, childhood, adolescence
and obsolescence.
(Art Linkletter)

There are three signs of old age: you forget names, you forget faces, and...
(Red Skelton)

We were planning to count the candles on his birthday cake, but we were driven back by the heat.
(Stuart Turner)

I'm at the age where just
putting my cigarette in the
holder is a thrill.
(George Burns)

34

And then there was the woman who said on her 100th birthday, 'I feel quite well, despite the fact that my youngest son has just gone into an old folks home'.

When a man of 60 runs of
with a young woman I wish
him luck. After all he's going to
need it.
(Deborah Kerr)

He's so old; his birth certificate
is carved on a ROCK.
(Jack Benny)

Except for an occasional heart attack I feel as young as I ever did.
(Robert Benchley)

Retirement at 65 is ridiculous.
At 65 I still had pimples
(George Burns)

Getting on in years means
suffering the morning after
when you haven't even had the
night before.
(Henny Youngman)

If you live long enough you get accused of things you never did, and praised for virtues you never had!
(I.F. Stone)

All would live long, but none would be old. (Benjamin Franklin)

An old man gives good advice to console himself for no longer being able to set a bad example.
(Duc de la Rochefoucauld)

The tragedy of old age is not that one is old, but that one is young.
(Mark Twain)

He was either a man of about 150 who was rather young for his years or a man of about 110 who had been aged by trouble. (P.G Wodehouse)

If you can eat a boiled egg at 90 in England they think you deserve the Nobel Prize.
(Alan Bennett)

Anyone can get old. All you
have to do is live long enough
(Groucho Marx)

If I'd known I was going to live this long I'd have taken better care of myself.
(Adolph Zukor)

There are certain signs that you're getting on in years. I walked past the cemetery the other day and two guys ran after me with shovels.
(Rodney Dangerfield)

49

He's so old; his blood type has
been discontinued.
(Bill Dana)

I would say I was 99, dahling. (Zsa Zsa Gabor; after being asked what she would do if she lived to be 100)

It is obscene to think that one day one will look like an old map of France.
(Brigitte Bardot)

Nowadays when a fan runs up to me it's not to get my autograph but to have a better look at my wrinkles.
(Liz Taylor)

First you forget names, then you forget faces. Then you forget to zip your fly. Then you forget to unzip your fly. (American baseball manager Branch Rickey on the perils of ageing)

Growing old is something you do
if you're lucky,
(Groucho Marx)

When you're green you're growing, when you're ripe you're not.
(Ray Kroc)

In youth we run into
difficulties. In old age,
difficulties run into us.
(Josh Billings)

You know you're getting old
when the candles cost more
than the cake.
(Bob Hope)

58

Every morning when I get up, I read the obituary page. If my name isn't in it, I shave.
(George Burns)

I'm 65 and I guess that puts me in with the geriatrics. But if there were 15 months in every year, I'd only be 48. That's the trouble with us. We number everything. Take women for example. I think they deserve to have more than twelve years between the ages of 28 and 40. (James Thurber)

The three ages of man are young, old and "You're looking wonderful"!
(Jack Lynch)

You're only as old as the
woman you're feeling.
(Groucho Marx)

I am just turning forty, and taking my time about it. (Comedian Harold Lloyd after being asked his age when he was 77)

I'm so old I knew Madame Butterfly when she was a caterpillar.
(Bob Hope)

After the age of 80, everything reminds you of something else.
(Lowell Thomas)

I recently turned 60. Practically
a third of my life is over.
(Woody Allen)

When you're old, everything you do is sort of a miracle.
(Millicent Fenwick)

When we speak about people of a 'certain age,' what we mean is people of an UN-certain age.

If you want to make a success of old age you have to start young.
(Fred Astaire)

I've got to the age where I need my false teeth and my hearing aid before I can ask where I've left my glasses.
(Stuart Turner)

He's so old that when he orders
a 3-minute egg, they ask for
the money upfront.
(Milton Berle)

There are three signs of old age. Loss of memory. I forget the other two.
(Red Skelton)

The only thing that bothers me about growing older is that when I see a pretty girl now it arouses my memory instead of my hopes.
(Milton Berle)

The secret of longevity is to
keep breathing.
(Sophie Tucker)

Bob Hope needs the year
between his birthdays to get
the wind up to blow out all the
candles on his cake.

She's a woman of a certain age
-the Stone Age.

There are so many ways of dying. It's astonishing that any of us choose old age.
(Beryl Bainbridge)

The hardest years in life are
between 10 and 70.
(Helen Hayes)

Men come of age at sixty,
women at fifteen.
(James Stephens)

By the time you reach my age
you've made plenty of mistakes
if you've lived your life properly.
(Ronald Reagan)

She claims she just turned 30: it must have been a U-turn.

Allow me to put the record straight. I'm 46 and have been for some years past.
(Erica Jong)

You know you're getting old when everything hurts. And what doesn't hurt doesn't work.
(Hy Gardner)

The older I get, the better I used
to be.
(John McEnroe)

I'm now at the age where I've got to prove that I'm just as good as I never was.
(Rex Harrison)

I'm at the age where my back
goes out more than I do.
(Phyllis Diller)

People ought to retire at 40 when they feel over-used and go back to work at 65 when they feel useless.
(Carol Anne O'Marie)

You know you're getting older
when you try to straighten out
the wrinkles in your socks -and
discover you're not wearing
any.
(Leonard Knott)

At my age, the only reason I'd take up jogging again would be to hear heavy breathing.
(Erma Bombeck)

I refuse to admit I'm more than 52 even if that makes my sons illegitimate.
(Nancy Astor)

I wish I could tell you my age
but it's impossible. It keeps
changing all the time.
(Greer Garson)

You're getting old when the only thing you don't want for your birthday is to be reminded of it.

You know you're getting old when everything hurts. And what doesn't hurt doesn't work.
(Hy Gardner)

You can order other Little books directly from Powerfresh Limited. All at £2.50 each including postage (UK only)

Postage and packing outside the UK: Europe: add 20% of retail price
Rest of the world: add 30% of retail price

To order any Powerfresh book please call 0845 130 4565

Powerfresh Limited
21 Rothersthorpe Crescent
Northampton NN4 8JD